2/04

Landmark
Events in
American
History

The Oregon Trail

Michael V. Uschan

WORLD ALMANAC® LIBRARY

Dedication
To Joshua T. Horton—Happy Trails

Please visit our web site at: www.worldalmanaclibrary.com
For a free color catalog describing World Almanac® Library's list of high-quality
books and multimedia programs, call 1-800-848-2928 (USA) or 1-800-387-3178
(Canada). World Almanac® Library's fax: (414) 332-3567.

Library of Congress Cataloging-in-Publication Data

Uschan, Michael V., 1948-
    The Oregon trail / by Michael V. Uschan.
      p. cm. — (Landmark events in American history)
    Includes bibliographical references and index.
    Summary: Examines the famous westward route of American settlement during the 1800s, including
everyday life on the trail, what it took to make the journey successfully, and what happened to unsuccessful
attempts to reach the Oregon Territory.
    ISBN 0-8368-5386-5 (lib. bdg.)
    ISBN 0-8368-5414-4 (softcover)
    1. Oregon National Historic Trail—History—Juvenile literature. 2. Overland journeys to the Pacific—
Juvenile literature. 3. Frontier and pioneer life—West (U.S.)—Juvenile literature. 4. Pioneers—West
(U.S.)—History—19th century—Juvenile literature. 5. Northwest, Pacific—History—19th century—
Juvenile literature. 6. West (U.S.)—History—19th century—Juvenile literature. [1. Oregon National
Historic Trail. 2. Frontier and pioneer life—West (U.S.). 3. Pioneers. 4. Overland journeys to the Pacific.
5. West (U.S.)—Social life and customs.] I. Title. II. Series.
    F597.U83 2004
    917.804'2—dc22
                                      2003061389

First published in 2004 by
World Almanac® Library
330 West Olive Street, Suite 100
Milwaukee, WI 53212 USA

Copyright © 2004 by World Almanac® Library.

Produced by Discovery Books
Editor: Sabrina Crewe
Designer and page production: Sabine Beaupré
Photo researcher: Sabrina Crewe
Maps and diagrams: Stefan Chabluk
World Almanac® Library editorial direction: Mark J. Sachner
World Almanac® Library art direction: Tammy Gruenewald
World Almanac® Library production: Jessica Morris

Photo credits: Corbis: pp. 5, 6, 10, 11, 12, 13, 14, 16, 18, 19, 21, 23, 25, 32, 34, 35, 37,
38, 40, 41, 42; The Granger Collection: p. 28; North Wind Picture Archives: cover, pp. 7,
8, 9, 15, 17, 20, 24, 26, 27, 29, 30, 31. 33, 36, 39, 43.

Printed in the United States of America

1 2 3 4 5 6 7 8 9 08 07 06 05 04

Contents

Introduction

A Famous Trail

In the mid-nineteenth century, the Oregon Trail was the only practical path on which Americans could travel west of the Rocky Mountains. Starting in the early 1840s, many thousands of people used the trail. It began in Independence, Missouri, and snaked westward more than 2,000 miles (3,200 kilometers) across rolling **plains**, high deserts, and snow-capped mountains.

The route was named the Oregon Trail because it ended in what was, in the early nineteenth century, called Oregon Country. This huge area in the Pacific Northwest sprawled westward from the Rocky Mountains to the Pacific Ocean and north from California into what is now Canada. The name of the trail is misleading, however, because the Oregon Trail was used not just to reach Oregon but to get to California, Utah, and other areas.

This map shows how the United States extended its borders over time. The Oregon Trail helped settlers reach the new western territory.

KEY
Extent of U.S. in 1783
Extent of U.S in 1803
Extent of U.S in 1819
Extent of U.S in 1846
Extent of U.S in 1853
Present-day state boundaries

An Expanding Nation

When the United States was founded in 1776, it consisted of thirteen states hugging the coast of the Atlantic Ocean. In a treaty signed with Britain in 1783, however, the young nation gained ownership of land as far west as the Mississippi River. In 1803, the United States doubled its size with the Louisiana Purchase, in which it bought from France a huge area of land that extended westward from the Mississippi River to the Rocky Mountains. Several decades later, the Oregon Trail would help the United States extend its borders even farther, to the Pacific Ocean.

A Difficult Route

By wagon, on horseback, and on foot, traveling on the Oregon Trail entailed a host of dangers and hardships, including disease, shortages of food and water, and occasional attacks by Indians. Despite the many hazards and difficulties, however, people continued to venture along the Oregon Trail in search of land and a better life in the **West**. The trail was a key factor in encouraging settlement across the North American continent.

On their journey west, travelers on the Oregon Trail stopped at Independence Rock in Wyoming. There, thousands of them etched their names and the date into the rock's side.

Enduring the Trail

"A man must be able to endure heat like a salamander, mud and water like a muskrat, dust like a toad, and labor like a jackass. He must learn to eat with his unwashed fingers, sleep on the ground when it rains, and share his blanket with vermin. He must cease to think, except as to where he may find grass and water and a good camping place."

A traveler comments on the hardships of the Oregon Trail, 1852

Chapter 1

Oregon Country

Native Peoples of the Northwest

Oregon Country was an area in the Pacific Northwest that would one day yield the states of Oregon, Washington, and Idaho, parts of Montana and Wyoming, and Canada's British Columbia. The first white people arriving there discovered that it was rich in animal life, rivers and lakes, and dense forests, making it a desirable place for settlement. Indeed, it was already settled by many Native American tribes. Oregon Country had been inhabited for more than ten thousand years by the time Europeans came there.

The tribes had established varying traditions, ways of life, and languages. Peoples such as the Chinook, Clatsop, Tillamook, and Tlingit located their villages along the ocean shore or on nearby off-shore islands. Most of what they ate, including whales and seals, came from the sea.

Living to the east—in an area of heavy forests, mountains, and many rivers and streams—were the Cayuse, Coeur D'Alene,

This area of Olympic National Park in the state of Washington gives an idea of how Oregon Country appeared before white settlement. Oregon's fertile lands and waters made it suitable for farming, forestry, and fishing.

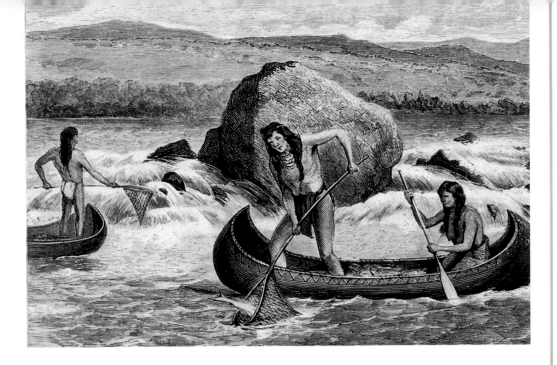

The peoples of the Northwest were superb canoe builders and skillful fishermen who depended on the ocean and rivers for their food. These people are fishing for salmon on the Columbia River.

Flathead, Nez Percé, Walla Walla, and Yakama. These tribes depended on salmon, trout, and other fish for most of their food.

Oregon peoples also hunted deer and bear and gathered wild foods, such as berries, but they did not plant food crops. They all trapped animals, including sea otter, fox, and beaver, for their furs. It was these furs that led to the Indians' first contacts with whites in Oregon Country.

The Arrival of Europeans

The first Europeans to arrive in Oregon Country came by ship. The Spanish, while settling California to the south, sailed along the coast as early as 1543. Sir Francis Drake of England explored the area in

A Mystery Name

The origin of the name "Oregon," in use since the late 1700s, remains a mystery. Oregon—sometimes spelled Ouragon—was the name for the Columbia River until 1792, when American sea captain Robert Gray renamed it after his ship. The first known written use of the word was by Major Robert Rogers, who in 1765 proposed exploring "Ouragon" country. Historians believe it is a variation of a word spoken by one of the area's early explorers. It may have come from the French-Canadian word ouragan, meaning "storm" or "hurricane"; from the Spanish orejon, which means "big-ear," a term applied to some tribes; or from the Spanish orégano, for the wild sage that grows in the area. But no one knows for sure how Oregon got its name.

1578. The Russians, who had already started colonizing what would become Alaska, began visiting in the early 1700s in search of furs to sell in Europe.

In March 1778, English Captain James Cook—who is famous for exploring the Hawaiian Islands—landed on the central Oregon coast. Cook traded brass buttons and other cheap trinkets for sea otter pelts, which he sold in China.

Americans and British Stake Their Claims

The first Americans were led by Robert Gray, a ship's captain from Boston. He and his crew stepped ashore at Tillamook Bay on

Introducing Change

In the eighteenth and early nineteenth centuries, European and American explorers and fur traders in Oregon Country introduced new tools and goods to the people living there. In return for furs, Indians received not only flashy trinkets such as bright beads, but cloth, steel knives, fish hooks, iron pots for cooking, and guns for hunting and warfare. These new items began to change the way the Indians lived. And because they could not make such items themselves, Native Americans who had once been self-sufficient became dependent on white traders.

Fur traders used these beads to exchange with Native hunters for furs.

8

May 14, 1788, to trade for furs. On May 11, 1792, Gray returned, and his ship, the *Columbia Rediviva*, became the first to enter the mouth of what is now the Columbia River.

Gray named the river after his ship, the *Columbia*, and claimed the area for the United States. But just a few months later, in October, Captain George Vancouver also sailed into the Columbia River and claimed the Pacific Northwest for Britain. The two nations would compete for control of Oregon Country for the next half century.

Lewis and Clark

On November 7, 1805, William Clark penned the following entry in his journal: "Ocian in view! O! the joy." The "Ocian" Clark referred to was the Pacific Ocean. Clark, Meriwether Lewis, and other members of the Corps of Discovery had become the first white Americans to travel across North America after President Thomas Jefferson dispatched them to explore the huge territory west of the Mississippi River and all the way to the Pacific.

Lewis and Clark's long, difficult journey across the West began May 1804, in St. Louis, Missouri. The expedition reached the Pacific Ocean in early November and spent the winter at the mouth of the Columbia with the Clatsop tribe. They built a rough

President Jefferson instructed Lewis and Clark to record in detail everything they saw. The expedition came across many plants and animals not previously seen by white people— this is a page from Clark's records describing a pheasant.

The Mission of Lewis and Clark

"The object of your mission is to explore the Missouri River and such principal streams of it, as, by its course and communication with the waters of the Pacific Ocean, may offer the most direct & practicable [travel route] across this continent for the purposes of commerce."

President Thomas Jefferson's instructions to Lewis and Clark, 1803

wooden shelter to live in, naming it Fort Clatsop. On March 23, 1806, the explorers headed home, returning to St. Louis on September 23.

The reports brought back by Lewis and Clark made Americans aware of the vast new land to the west, including Oregon Country. The most exciting discovery was Clark's claim that the region was "richer in beaver and otter than any country on earth." This promise of riches to be made in the fur trade ignited a stampede of trappers westward to the Rocky Mountains and Oregon Country.

Fort Astoria was built at the point where the Columbia River runs into the Pacific Ocean. The first permanent U.S. settlement in the region, it survives today as the town of Astoria.

Fur Trappers Arrive

In 1811, employees of New York businessman John Jacob Astor's Pacific Fur Company built Fort Astoria on the Columbia River near the ruins of Fort Clatsop. In 1824, the powerful Hudson's Bay Company, a British firm, erected Fort Vancouver further inland on the Columbia's north bank. The fur trading companies from the United States and Britain had begun their battle for control of Oregon Country.

A Wild and Varied Landscape

"From the site of the establishment [Fort Astoria] the eye could wander over a varied and interesting scene. The extensive sound, with its rocky shores, lay in front; the breakers rolling in wild confusion, closed the view on the west; on the east, the country had a wild and varied aspect; while towards the south, the magnificent forest darkened the landscape as far as the eye could reach."

Alexander Ross, who helped build Fort Astoria in 1811

Fort Vancouver, the British rival to Fort Astoria, is on the right in this picture. Drawn in the 1850s, the picture shows that the site had by then become an established settlement. It is now the city of Vancouver, Washington.

Chapter 2

A Trail to the West

Ancient Trails

For thousands of years, Native Americans traveled across North America in search of new places to live. They were the first to discover hundreds of rivers, mountain passes, watering holes, and trails.

In the early 1800s, fur **trappers** and explorers began searching for routes across the continent. Although they claimed to be the first to discover new paths west, they were in fact journeying along trails already well used by Native Americans.

Mountain Men Map the Trail

In the 1820s and 1830s, the westward flow of fur trappers quickened because of a new fashion craze in the East: men's top hats made of beaver skins. The now-legendary mountain men, such as Kit Carson, Jedediah Smith, John Colter, James Beckwourth, and Jim Bridger, pursued their prey all over Oregon Country and the Rocky Mountains. They came across rivers, lakes, game trails, and mountain paths that made their

Every year, a huge *rendezvous* (a French word meaning "meeting") was held, usually in southern Wyoming. Mountain men and Native trappers traded with the fur companies, feasted, and competed in games.

James Bridger (1804—1881)

James (Jim) Bridger, one of the most colorful characters among the mountain men, made his first journey to the West when he joined an expedition to the Upper Missouri at the age of seventeen. From the 1820s to the 1830s, he worked as a trapper for various fur companies, including his own Rocky Mountain Fur Company.

In 1841, Bridger founded a trading post, located in the southwest corner of present-day Wyoming, on the path to the West that would become the Oregon Trail. Within a short space of time, Fort Bridger was flourishing as an important stopping place for **emigrants**, who would arrive exhausted and short of supplies.

Back in 1824, Bridger had been one of the first whites to come across the Great Salt Lake, and he later advised **Mormon** leader Brigham Young on settlement of the area. By 1853, the Mormons had control of Utah **Territory**, which included Fort Bridger, and Bridger was edged out, eventually selling the fort to the Mormons. In 1855, Bridger bought a farm near Kansas City, where he died at the age of seventy-seven.

journeys easier. Over time, their routes would be woven together into the Oregon Trail.

Finding a Pass

The most significant discovery was made by Robert Stuart of the Pacific Fur Company. Stuart was on a supply trip from Fort Astoria to St. Louis, Missouri, on October 22, 1812. While following a Crow Indian trail through the Rocky Mountains, he found a **pass** so wide and flat that horses and wagons could cross through it. It

Robert Stuart kept the pass he found a secret from other fur companies, but the Crows showed it to Jedediah Smith in 1823. After that, South Pass (so named because it was south of where Lewis and Clark had crossed the mountains) became an established route over the Rocky Mountains.

led over the mountains down to the **Great Plains**, forming a natural bridge between east and west for those traveling the Oregon Trail. The pass came to be known as South Pass.

A Way for Wagons

In 1830, mountain men led by Jedediah Smith left St. Louis with ten wagons loaded with supplies for trappers. Smith led them over South Pass, and it was the first time wagons traveled all the way west over the Rocky Mountains. The *St. Louis Beacon* newspaper later claimed this transportation feat proved settlers could journey to Oregon Country, something that had previously been thought impossible because they would need wagons to carry supplies and personal possessions.

Easy Crossing
"The ease with which they did it and [the fact they] could have gone on to the mouth of the Columbia, shows the folly and nonsense of those "scientific" characters who talk of the Rocky Mountains as the barrier which will stop the westward march of the American people."

Newspaper story about fur trapper wagons crossing the Rockies, St. Louis Beacon, *1830*

A wagon train from the East heads west, carrying supplies to Oregon Country. The supply trains of the early 1830s proved that wagons could make it over the Rocky Mountains.

Potential for Business

In the early 1830s, other Americans began to follow the trappers west. Andrew J. Wyeth of Boston, Massachusetts, reached Fort Vancouver in 1832 to start the Columbia River Fishing and Trading Company. His business of buying furs and salmon for sale back east failed, but Wyeth's efforts led other businessmen and political leaders to realize the new area's potential. Two years later, Wyeth built Fort Hall in Idaho, the first permanent U.S. **outpost** west of the Rocky Mountains.

The Book of Heaven

In October 1832, four Indians from Oregon Country—three Nez Percés and one Flathead—arrived in St. Louis, Missouri, with a band of fur trappers. In a meeting with William Clark, the famous explorer who was now Superintendent of Indian Affairs, the Indians said they had traveled over a thousand miles to learn about the white man's "Book of Heaven" (the Bible). When the story of the Indians' curiosity about the Bible was reported in 1833 in the *Christian Advocate and Journal*, it ignited a wave of interest among **missionaries**. They began to travel to Oregon Country in an attempt to convert Indians to Christianity.

A Mission in the West

The other set of newcomers did not want to make money—their goal was to convert Indians to Christianity. In 1834, Methodist Reverend Jason Lee traveled west with Wyeth, who was returning to pursue his financial dream. Lee continued on to the lush Willamette Valley in Oregon Country, where he built a house and chapel on the Willamette River. His successful journey inspired other missionaries to follow him there.

The Pend D'Oreille mission in the Rocky Mountains, shown here, was built by Christians hoping to make converts among the Native peoples of Oregon Country.

The Whitmans

Two Presbyterian missionary couples—Marcus and Narcissa Whitman and Henry and Eliza Spalding—set out from western

Buffalo Meat

"Not one in our number relishes buffalo meat as well as my husband and I. He has a different way for cooking every piece of meat. We have meat and tea in the morn, and tea and meat at noon. All our variety consists of the different ways of cooking. I relish it well and it agrees with me. My health is excellent. I never saw any thing like buffalo meat to satisfy hunger."

Narcissa Whitman, journal entry, 1836

New York State in 1836. Whitman and Spalding were the first white women to travel the Oregon Trail. The fact that they survived the rugged journey and made the trip in a wagon was proof that families could use this new route to **migrate** west, a key factor in boosting westward travel.

Although the trip was rough, Narcissa Whitman loved it. "I never was so contented and happy before, neither have I enjoyed such health for years," she wrote in a daily journal that has become one of the classic accounts of the Oregon Trail.

The four missionaries eventually arrived in the Willamette Valley and established a **mission** for the Cayuse, Nez Percé, and Flathead tribes. Their experiences on the Oregon Trail—eating buffalo meat, meeting Indians, and straining to haul wagons over the mountains—would be duplicated thousands of times in the following decades by families making the journey in wagon trains.

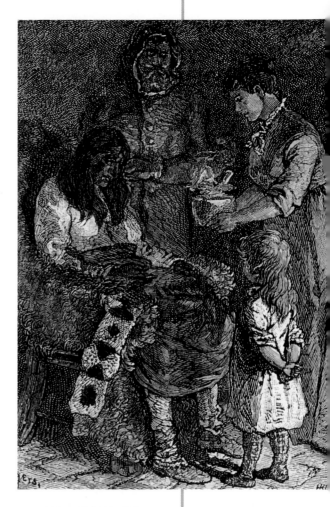

Narcissa Whitman brings soup to a sick person at the Whitmans' mission in the Willamette Valley. She and her husband ran their mission until they were killed in 1846 (see page 38).

Painting Oregon Country

In 1837, a painter named Alfred Jacob Miller accompanied British adventurer William Drummond Stewart and American Fur Company trappers to the Rocky Mountains. In the spring of 1839, an exhibition was held in New York City of Miller's paintings from his trip. The imagery thrilled the thousands of people who flocked to see Miller's huge, dramatic oil paintings of Indians, buffalo hunts, mountain men, landscapes, and other sights along the Oregon Trail. The colorful scenes in Miller's paintings (see page 32) made people want to head west and see the sights for themselves.

Fever and Destiny

In the 1840s, two powerful movements in U.S. society—Oregon Fever and **Manifest** Destiny—began to infect the United States. The heated emotions and passionate desires created by these twin forces propelled the nation into a war for new territory. It also sent tens of thousands of people streaming westward along the Oregon Trail in search of new homes.

Manifest Destiny

In an 1845 editorial in the *United States Magazine and Democratic Review*, John L. O'Sullivan coined a famous phrase that captured the nation's growing desire for more territory. O'Sullivan wrote, "It is our Manifest Destiny to overspread the continent allotted by Providence for the free development of our yearly multiplying millions." The idea caught on,

The idea of Manifest Destiny was depicted in many illustrations and paintings of the middle to late 1800s. Images such as this Currier and Ives print showed white civilization—in the form of houses, wagons, and trains—spreading westward while the Native people move aside.

despite the fact that Mexico controlled California and much of the Southwest, the British were still contesting ownership of Oregon Country, and Native Americans lived throughout the West.

In 1844, Democrat James K. Polk was elected president of the United States, largely because his party favored **westward expansion**. The United States and Britain had agreed to joint ownership of Oregon Country in 1818. As Polk noted in 1845, however, an estimated five thousand U.S. citizens already lived there compared to fewer than a thousand British. He pronounced, "Our title [claim] to the country of the Oregon is clear and unquestionable. Already are our people preparing to perfect that title by occupying it with their wives and children."

President James Polk made Manifest Destiny a reality. During his presidency, Oregon, California, and the Southwest became U.S. territory, adding the western third of the North American continent to the United States' possessions.

What Created Oregon Fever?

"Oregon Fever" was the term given to the craze for moving west in the 1840s—it swept the nation and overcame sensible fears of a long, difficult journey. Several factors in the early 1840s combined to promote Oregon Fever. Economic depressions in 1837 and 1841 had burdened many eastern farms with big debts, and some farmers had lost their property. By going west, they could acquire new land that was cheap or free and in a place with a good climate and rich soil. The arrival of thousands of foreign **immigrants** in the East had made good, cheap, land scarce, and the cities were becoming increasingly crowded and dirty. There were also glowing reports from people who had already moved to Oregon, such as Marcus Whitman, or the settler who claimed Oregon Country was "a **pioneer**'s paradise."

19

The distant dream that sparked Oregon Fever was that of a farm in the West. This was Polk County, Oregon, in the 1880s, where farmland abounded.

The Great Migration

The flow of newcomers to Oregon Country was slow to pick up. Only a few hundred settlers arrived in 1841 and 1842. The trickle of emigrants along the Oregon Trail grew to a flood in 1843, however, when 1,000 people made the trek. Leading them was Marcus Whitman, the missionary who had traveled the trail in its infancy. In 1844, 1,400 people headed west. This number more than doubled in 1845, when 3,000 emigrants traveled the Oregon Trail. The movement of people west soon became known as "the Great Migration."

New Opportunities

"He said he wanted us all to go with him to the new country. He had talked about Oregon and the Columbia River for many years. He wanted to take his nine sons where they could get land."

Martha Gay, thirteen years old, writing of her father's decision to leave Springfield, Missouri, 1851

Agreeing to a Border

The arrival of so many white American settlers in Oregon Country strengthened the idea of Manifest Destiny. U.S. officials began to demand that the British leave what they claimed was clearly a U.S. possession. The 1844 campaign slogan that helped elect Polk was "Fifty-four forty or fight," a reference to the latitude line—54°40' north—that marked the desired northern border of the United States with British Canada.

When the United States and Britain agreed on a new border on June 18, 1846, however, Polk settled for less territory than he had first demanded. The line between the two countries was drawn at 49° north, several hundred miles south of 54°40'. The reason Polk was willing to relinquish part of Oregon Country was that the United States was already at war with another nation over a much larger territory. The opponent was Mexico, and the prize was California and the Southwest.

A cartoon published during the Oregon debate shows the Americans threatening to fight if they don't get the territory they want. The original caption had the British character (left) saying, "What, you young Yankee-noodle, strike your own father?"

The Mexican War

Shortly before Polk had taken office in 1845, outgoing President John Tyler had **annexed** Texas, a republic created in 1836 by

Wanting it All

"Make way, I say, for the American Buffalo—he has not yet got land enough. I tell you, we will give him Oregon for his summer shade and the region of Texas as his winter pasture. Like all of his race, he wants salt too. Well, he shall have the use of two oceans—the mighty Pacific and turbulent Atlantic shall be his."

A spokesman at the New Jersey State Democratic Convention, 1844

21

This map shows the West in 1848, two years after the boundary was drawn through Oregon Country to divide the British part from the U.S. part. It also shows how the Mormon and California Trails departed from the Oregon Trail, one taking travelers to Utah and the other leading to the gold fields.

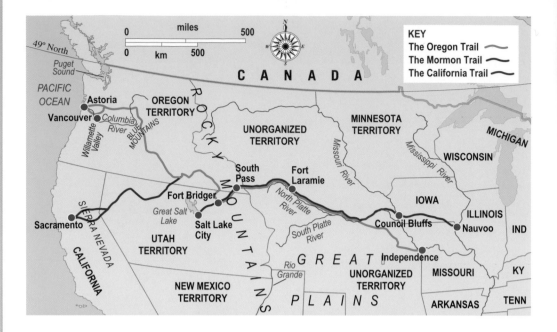

Different Routes and Names

Before becoming known as the Oregon Trail, the route had other names: originally called simply the "trapper's route," it became known as the Emigrant Road in the early 1840s. After 1845, it was also referred to as the Oregon and California Trail and then eventually just as the Oregon Trail.

People who traveled the Oregon Trail were not just going to Oregon Country. Everyone heading west had to begin the trip on this famous and important trail because it was the only route over the Rocky Mountains. Two other trails, however, split off from the Oregon Trail after it crossed that range. Settlers who wanted to go to California left the Oregon Trail in Idaho and began journeying southwest along the California Trail to reach their destination. For this reason, the Oregon Trail became heavily traveled after gold was discovered in California in 1848. In 1846, thousands of Mormons began journeying west to their new home in Utah Territory. The Mormon Trail split off to the south from the Oregon Trail after Fort Bridger in present-day Wyoming, then a major stop for emigrants to rest and get fresh supplies.

U.S. citizens rebelling against Mexican rule. The annexation infuriated Mexico, which still claimed a part of Texas.

Disputes over Texas led to the Mexican War, which began on May 13, 1846, when U.S. forces began an invasion of Mexico, the Southwest, and California. The war ended with a victory for the United States after it captured Mexico City in 1847. In the 1848 Treaty of Hidalgo signed after the war, the United States received California and a large area that would become the states of Nevada and Utah, most of Arizona and New Mexico, and part of Colorado.

A Dream Realized

With the acquisition of Oregon Country and California, the United States had realized the grand goal of Manifest Destiny—to occupy North America from one coast to another. It was now that the Oregon Trail began to play its vital role in U.S. history. Americans had to populate the new western lands they had won, and the steady flow of travelers along the Oregon Trail would accomplish this in just a few decades.

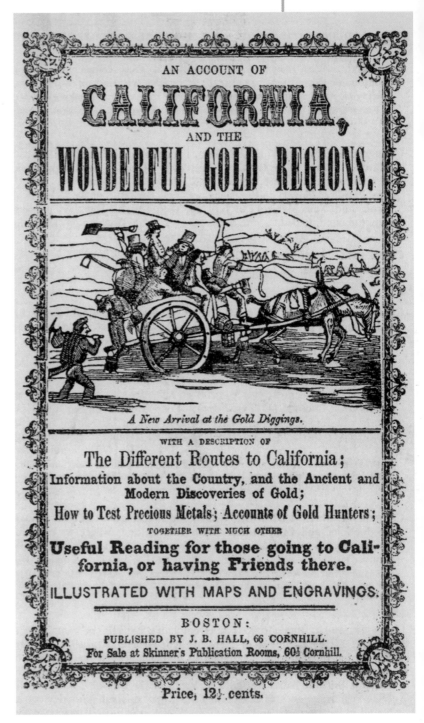

AN ACCOUNT OF

CALIFORNIA,

AND THE

WONDERFUL GOLD REGIONS.

A New Arrival at the Gold Diggings.

WITH A DESCRIPTION OF

The Different Routes to California;

Information about the Country, and the Ancient and Modern Discoveries of Gold;

How to Test Precious Metals; Accounts of Gold Hunters;

TOGETHER WITH MUCH OTHER

Useful Reading for those going to California, or having Friends there.

ILLUSTRATED WITH MAPS AND ENGRAVINGS.

BOSTON:
PUBLISHED BY J. B. HALL, 66 CORNHILL.
For Sale at Skinner's Publication Rooms, 60½ Cornhill.

Price, 12½ cents.

The number of people using the Oregon Trail was dramatically boosted by the discovery of gold in California in 1848. By 1849, thousands were heading west along the Oregon and California Trails to seek their fortunes.

Chapter 4

Traveling the Oregon Trail

Wagon Trains

The journey west along the Oregon Trail took between four and six months. The trail itself began on the outskirts of Independence, Missouri. It was there—or in other Missouri towns such as Council Bluffs and St. Joseph—that emigrants gathered each spring to form groups called wagon trains.

Wagon trains could number from a few dozen wagons to hundreds. The members of the group would stick together throughout the journey—it was safest to travel in wagon trains because it made it easier to cope with difficult parts of the trip, such as crossing rivers. Being in a large group also helped when emigrants became ill, ran out of food or water, or had problems with their wagons.

Prairie Schooners

The wagons that traveled the Oregon Trail were nicknamed "prairie **schooners**" because of their high, rounded, white covers that reminded people of sails on ships. Wagons were generally 4 feet (1.2 meters) wide, 10–12 feet (3–4 m) long, and about 10 feet (3 m) high. The wagons weighed some 1,300 pounds (590 kg) empty and could carry approximately 3,000 pounds (1,360 kg). The bed of the wagon was piled high with supplies, and at night it also served as sleeping quarters. Its bottom was usually sealed with tar, making it watertight so it could float across a river. A wagon had front wheels smaller than those in the rear to make it easier to maneuver. The wooden wheels were rimmed with iron to protect them from rocks and rough terrain.

Along the Oregon Trail, there were trading posts that catered to the needs of those who ran out of supplies on the long journey. This is a replica of the store at Fort Laramie as it appeared when it served emigrants in the 1840s.

Wagon trains were usually guided by former mountain men. Before starting, members of wagon trains elected other leaders as well: a captain and officers to make daily decisions, such as where to camp each night. They also approved general rules—for instance that every man had to stand guard duty. On some wagon trains, gambling and drinking liquor were banned.

Most emigrants chose oxen to pull wagons, even though they were slower than horses. Their pace was only 2 miles (3.2 km) an hour, but oxen cost less, Indians were less likely to steal them, and they were dependable. Emigrant Peter Burnett hailed the ox as "a most noble animal, patient, thrifty, durable, gentle [and with] more genuine hardihood and pluck than either mules or horses."

Bare Necessities

Travelers filled their wagons with basic supplies—food, clothing, cooking pots, tools, medicine, spare parts for wagons, and personal belongings. To reach the Pacific Northwest, a family of four needed 1,000 pounds (450 kilograms) of food, including some 150 pounds (70 kg) of bacon and 200 pounds (90 kg) of flour. Most also started with a few cattle and some chickens and pigs, all of which could be eaten along the way.

Every family had at least one gun for protection and for hunting buffalo and other animals. In an 1845 travel guide, pioneer

Lansford Hastings advised emigrants to come well armed: "All persons should, invariably, equip themselves with a good gun, at least 5 pounds (2.3 kg) of [gun]powder, and 20 pounds (9 kg) of lead [for bullets]."

Daily Life on the Trail

The men, women, and children who made the long, difficult trip over the Oregon Trail would leave Missouri in April or May. Their spring departure was timed to coincide with the grass on the Plains growing long enough to feed their livestock along the way.

Travelers made slow progress on the Oregon Trail, what with herding livestock and moving wagons loaded down with possessions. They usually traveled between 10 and 20 miles (16 and 32 km) in a day.

A day on the trail started before first light, around 4:00 A.M., sometimes to the accompaniment of a rifle shot. Travelers made a fire to cook breakfast, often using dried buffalo droppings for fuel because wood was scarce. They often ate sowbelly and slam-johns (bacon and pancakes), a meal they might have day after day.

The Cost of Emigration

A trip on the Oregon Trail was not cheap. It required a minimum of $500 and as much as $1,000 to purchase a wagon, animals, and food and supplies for the long journey. Those amounts seem small today, but in the middle of the nineteenth century, even $500 was a large sum of money. At the peak of emigration along the Oregon Trail—in about 1850—that $500 would be equal to approximately $11,500 today. Many families had trouble raising even the bare minimum required to pay for such a trip.

A large wagon train makes its camp on the Plains before heading into the mountains.

Emigrant Helen Carpenter once joked that "about the only change [in diet] we have from bread and bacon, is bacon and bread."

As the sun rose, people hitched oxen to their wagons and began moving west in a long line. Almost everyone walked because the wagons were so heavily loaded. They would stop around noon for lunch and then continue on until dark, when they would form a protective circle with their wagons and set up camp.

Crossing Rivers

The journey began easily enough, as emigrants followed the Platte River across the flat Great Plains. Even on the Plains, however, it was difficult to ford rivers, sometimes swollen by rain. Hundreds of people drowned in the Platte, Kansas, and Columbia Rivers. The emigrants usually floated their wagons across, with people

No Water, No Grass

"The last of the Black Hills we crossed this afternoon, over the roughest and most desolate piece of ground that was ever made (called by some the Devil's Crater). Not a drop of water, nor a spear of grass to be seen, nothing but barren hills, bare broken rock, sand and dust. We reached Platte River about noon, and our cattle were so crazy for water that some of them plunged head long into the river. Traveled 18 miles [29 km] and camp[ed]."

Emigrant Amelia Stewart Knight,
journal entry, 11 July 1853

27

A group of Sioux sit on the bank of the Platte River while emigrants head through Sioux homelands. Many lives and possessions were lost in the rivers along the Oregon Trail.

and animals sometimes having to swim. When crossing shallow water, animals, people, and wagons could become stuck in mud. In 1853, Rebecca Ketcham called the Vermillion River in Kansas "the worst stream we have crossed [because] the banks are so steep and muddy and rocky."

The Donner-Reed Party

There was always the risk on the journey west of being caught in the mountains during early snowfalls. In late October 1846, this calamity befell the Donner-Reed Party (named after its two leaders). This group of about ninety people, heading to California after traveling west on the Oregon Trail, became trapped in the Sierra Nevada when heavy snow started to fall.

Some of the stronger members of the party made it through deep snow over Truckee Pass (now named Donner Pass) to seek help, but it took a long time to get back. By mid-December, many of those left behind began dying of starvation—by the time rescuers finally arrived in February, forty-two people had died. To survive, others in the party had begun to eat the bodies of the dead.

Getting Through the Mountains

The trail became considerably harder as it entered the Rocky Mountains, climbed to South Pass, and then descended into what is today southern Idaho. After the Rockies, travelers on the California Trail had to negotiate the Sierra Nevada, and those emigrants bound for Oregon Country had to surmount the Blue Mountains.

It was backbreaking work to get wagons through the mountains. On the steepest parts of the trail, travelers combined their wagon teams because it took many animals to pull the wagons, one by one, up the mountain paths. The animals would then come back down, and the process was repeated for each wagon. People often had to lighten wagons by throwing out treasured possessions. It was always a sad task but one that was necessary to survive the journey.

As oxen strain to pull a wagon up the mountain path, a man pushes from behind. By the trail is the skeleton of an ox that didn't make it over the mountains.

Death on the Trail

Many emigrants, however, did not live to see the end of the Oregon Trail. Historians estimate that more than 34,000 people—at least 17 people for each mile (1.6 km) of the Oregon Trail—died while traveling. Emigrants died from thirst and starvation, drowning and other accidents, and attacks by Indians or robbers. Bad weather killed numbers of people: there were lightning strikes, fierce storms, flash floods, and sometimes drought conditions.

Thousands of people died on the journey west, most of them from illnesses for which there were no cures in the 1800s. These travelers' graves, marked by stones, lie along the Oregon Trail in southern Wyoming.

The major cause of death was illness, especially cholera, a disease that took more lives than any other single factor. There was no cure for cholera, which swept through entire wagon trains. It produced high fevers and vomiting and could kill a person in one day.

The Mormons

Members of the Church of Jesus Christ of the Latter Day Saints, known as the Mormons, began traveling the Oregon Trail in 1846, when church leader Brigham Young took the first group to their new home in Utah Territory.

The Mormons followed the Oregon Trail from Missouri, staying on the north side of the Platte

River so they would not meet emigrants of different faiths. After crossing the Rockies, they headed south on what became the Mormon Trail. In the first decade after Young reached Utah, more than sixty thousand Mormons joined him.

In the 1850s, the Mormon faith began attracting European immigrants. Most were so poor when they arrived in North America that they could not buy wagons. The solution was to push their belongings west in handcarts, and thousands of Mormons trekked to Utah this way. In 1856, three of five Mormon handcart companies made it through, but two started late and encountered bad winter weather. More than two hundred people died of the cold and starvation.

> **The Mormon Handcart Song**
> "Some must push and some must pull,
> As we go marching up the hill,
> So merrily on our way we go
> Until we reach the valley, O!"
>
> *Lyrics to a Mormon song*

Travel across the Great Plains became even more risky when the snows came. This group of Mormons, many on foot and pushing handcarts, struggled through terrible weather on their way to the newly founded Mormon capital of Salt Lake City.

Native Americans

The Oregon Trail sliced through the ancient homes of many peoples. The Pawnee, Sioux, and Cheyenne lived on the Great Plains, the Arapaho, Blackfeet, and Shoshone in the Rocky Mountains, and the Nez Percé and Cayuse in Oregon Country. The California and Mormon Trails also went through territory inhabited by many tribes.

Most encounters between emigrants and Native Americans were friendly. When the two groups met on the trail, they often traded for things needed by both sides, with emigrants offering clothes, tobacco, and iron tools in exchange for food or horses.

Over time, Indians began to resent whites trekking across their ancestral lands. Wagon trains became wary of theft because some groups of Indians stole horses and cattle. Attacks on wagon trains were rare, however. Historians estimate that between 1840 and 1860, only 360 emigrants were killed by Indians. About 400 Indians were killed in clashes, mainly because of the presence of the U.S. Army.

The outposts that dotted the West by the mid-1800s were right in the heart of Native homelands. This busy scene at Fort Laramie (painted by Alfred Jacob Miller after his 1837 trip to the West) shows Indians at the outpost when it was still a fur-trading center.

More and more U.S. soldiers were posted on the Plains and in the West as the 1800s progressed. Hostility turned to outright warfare when the U.S. Army decided to wipe out the western tribes and the Native Americans began to fight back.

Clash with the Sioux

In August 1854, a cow wandered away from a wagon train and ambled into a nearby Sioux village. The residents of the village killed and ate the cow. Thirty soldiers from Fort Laramie in present-day Wyoming, led by Lieutenant John Grattan, went to the village and demanded the tribe turn over the people who had killed the cow. When the Sioux refused, Grattan's men attacked, killing Chief Conquering Bear. The Sioux fought back, wiping out the detachment of soldiers. In retaliation, on September 3, 1854, six hundred soldiers from Fort Kearney in Nebraska attacked a Sioux encampment near Blue Water, killing eighty-five people and taking seventy women and children captive.

Giving Up

The hardships of the Oregon Trail proved too tough for some. They gave up in mid-journey and headed back east, winning the derisive nickname "go-backs." But most emigrants kept plodding along, hoping for a fine new home at the end of the Oregon Trail.

The End of the Trail

Willamette Valley in Oregon was where the first missions were founded in the region in the 1830s. It was settled by farmers in the 1800s and continues to be farmed today.

Arriving

Most of the people who journeyed over the Oregon Trail made the long, difficult trip for one reason: to find new homes for themselves. These 1843 diary entries from James W. Nesmith are typical of how these sturdy pioneers set to work after months of traveling: "Friday, October 27—Arrived at Oregon City at the falls of the Willamette." "Saturday, October 28—Went to work."

Whether it was in Oregon Country, California, Utah, or some other western destination, the first task of settlers was to secure some land. Often it was free for newcomers.

Hard Work

The end of the trip west meant the beginning of months and years of hard work. Most people started from scratch. They had to build their own homes and clear away trees and brush before planting corn, wheat, and other basic food crops.

Settlers who came in the later years could buy farms that already had cultivated fields and a house. The Knight family's journey began April 9, 1853, in Iowa and ended September 17 near what is now Milwaukie, Oregon. Amelia Stewart Knight's final entry in her journal of her trip explains how it concluded with a land purchase: "Here husband traded two yoke [pair] of oxen for land with one-half acre (0.20 hectare) planted to potatoes and a small log cabin no windows. This is the journey's end."

Creating New States

The hundreds of thousands of men, women, and children who traveled the Oregon Trail did not just make new homes for themselves in Oregon Country and other western areas. They also helped push the nation's boundaries west to the Pacific and create new states.

After 1846, when the United States and Britain split Oregon Country, the growing number of settlers there began demanding that their new home be officially made a part of the United States. On August 18, 1848, Congress granted this wish by establishing Oregon Territory, an area that included the future states of Oregon, Washington, Idaho, and part of Montana.

It took time, however, for these frontier areas to become states. After gold was discovered at Sutter's Mill in 1848, tens of thousands of people had begun flocking to California. The right to acquire statehood depended on population, and the Gold Rush influx soon

A photograph, taken in Washington in about 1890, shows a typical homestead for emigrants arriving in the Northwest. People struggled to scrape a living out of small piece of land they cleared in the forest.

Towns sprang up as more and more emigrants arrived along the Oregon Trail and, later, by railroad. This is the main street of Walla Walla, Washington, in the 1890s.

boosted the population of California enough for it to become the nation's thirty-first state on September 9, 1850. That year, Oregon still had fewer than twelve thousand people; it did not become a state until February 14, 1859.

Settlement was even slower in other areas reached by Oregon Trail emigrants. But the thousands of people who traveled the trail helped create the states of Washington and Montana (both 1889), Idaho and Wyoming (both 1890), and Utah (1896).

The Settlement at Bush Prairie

Not many African Americans traveled the Oregon Trail, but one of the earliest arrivals in Oregon Country was George Washington Bush, a black veteran of the War of 1812. In 1844, Bush and Michael Simmons led a group of about twenty-five African Americans from Missouri to Oregon Country. Bush knew the area because he had been a fur trapper. The white settlers in the future state of Oregon did not want blacks, however, and Bush's party headed north of the Columbia River to Puget Sound, an area then controlled by the British. Their settlement there became known as Bush Prairie.

In 1846, the United States and Britain were negotiating a formal boundary for Oregon Country. Even though the United States had rejected the black settlers, their presence was suddenly useful to the Americans during those negotiations. Because the Bush Prairie group was originally from the United States, the U.S. government used that fact to strengthen its claim to what would become the state of Washington.

Disease and Conflict

Those new states were carved out of Native homelands, and the Indians did not always surrender their homelands without a fight. There was good reason for this. The white invasion was a disaster for the people of Oregon Country. In addition to seizing land and disrupting hunting and fishing, emigrants introduced diseases such as measles, chicken pox, and cholera that killed thousands, sometimes wiping out whole tribes.

Narcissa and Marcus Whitman had arrived in Oregon Country in 1836 to establish a mission near the base of the Blue Mountains. As the years went by, Narcissa Whitman noted that the Cayuse, Umatilla, and Nez Percé Indians she dealt with were becoming dismayed by how many whites were moving into their homeland. "The poor Indians are amazed at the overwhelming numbers of

Native families of Oregon Country were devastated by white diseases to which they had no resistance. Like many Native people of the area, these Siwash people used sweat lodges to try to cure sickness. Rocks heated by the fire were put inside the small, dome-shaped structure to create a hot, steamy enclosure. There, a sick person would sit, hoping to sweat out his or her illness.

Americans coming into the country. They seem not to know what to make of it," she wrote.

In 1846, Cayuse children enrolled at the Whitmans' mission school in Wailatpu caught measles, igniting an **epidemic** that swept through their tribe. Indian leaders blamed the Whitmans for the deaths. Their anger increased when the Whitmans, who often doctored sick people, failed to save the sick Indians. On November 29, Chief Tilokaikt led a party that killed a dozen people, including the Whitmans, and kidnapped fifty white men, women, and children.

The Cayuse and Rogue River Wars

The incident opened the Cayuse War, Oregon Country's first significant outbreak of violence between Indians and whites. In the next few years, as punishment for the killings, the Cayuse were hunted down, defeated, and placed on **reservations**.

Many Cayuse people of Oregon ended up on the Umatilla Reservation, where this picture was taken by Edward Curtis in 1910. Curtis photographed this Cayuse woman in ceremonial dress as part of his extensive visual record of the vanishing Native peoples of North America.

From 1852 to 1856, whites and Indians fought a series of battles known as the Rogue River Wars. The wars ended with the defeat of all the tribes living in the Rogue and Umpqua valleys and along the southwestern Oregon coast. The tribes were then moved to reservations so that whites could take over the Native homelands.

Similar conflicts were occurring in the rest of Oregon Country and in other areas along the Oregon Trail. In the 1860s and the 1870s, the U.S. Army waged a campaign to protect settlers and to end the Indian resistance throughout the West.

The Last Defeat

The Nez Percé tribe had been friendly to whites since welcoming the Lewis and Clark expedition to Oregon Country in 1805. In 1877, the U.S. Army ordered Chief Joseph of the Nez Percé to take his band of eight hundred people from its traditional home near what is now the Washington-Idaho border to a reservation in present-day Idaho.

Instead, Joseph tried to lead his people to Canada, where he hoped they could live in freedom. The Army gave chase, and for four months the two sides waged a running battle across 2,000 miles (3,200 km) of Oregon, Washington, Idaho, and Montana.

Although Chief Joseph and his tribe won many of the fights against the more powerfully armed U.S. force, the long chase

For months, the U.S. Army pursued the Nez Percé all over the Northwest rather than let them escape to freedom in Canada.

Chief Joseph was leader of the Nez Percé when they were exiled from their homeland in spite of an 1855 U.S. **treaty** guaranteeing them their land forever. Another promise was broken by the U.S. government when the tribe surrendered. Instead of being sent to a reservation near their homelands, Chief Joseph's people were banished to Indian Territory, over 1,000 miles (1,600 km) away.

exhausted them and they ran out of food. Realizing that it was futile to continue to resist, Chief Joseph surrendered on October 5, 1877, near the Bear Paw Mountains of Montana. The eloquent speech Chief Joseph gave that day has come to symbolize the hopelessness Native Americans felt in trying to withstand the flood of white settlers who were taking their homes: "Hear me, my chiefs, I am tired; my heart is sick and sad. From where the sun now stands, I will fight no more forever."

Extinguishing the Buffalo

The buffalo is a symbol of the American West— a buffalo head once graced U.S. nickels— and when emigrants first began traveling the Oregon Trail, millions of them roamed the Great Plains. One of the most dramatic changes created by the coming of

whites was the destruction of these vast herds. Emigrants, trappers, and others shot them for sport or for their hides, leaving behind bleached bones and rotting meat. This wanton destruction was disastrous for Indian tribes that depended on buffalo for food, clothing, and other needs.

The worst of the slaughter happened during and after the construction of the Transcontinental Railroad, completed in 1869. Hunters shot buffalo by the thousand for meat to feed railroad workers. Later, passengers traveling by train across the country shot buffalo along the way, just as the emigrants on the Oregon Trail had done. By the 1880s, only a few thousand buffalo remained.

End of the Oregon Trail

The Oregon Trail itself was doomed by another historical event— the construction of the Transcontinental Railroad. The Union Pacific and Central Pacific Railroads connected their tracks at Promontory Summit, Utah, on May 10, 1869 to form the first rail route across the West. The Oregon Trail was no longer needed.

Emigrants began taking the railroad west because the trip was infinitely easier and much shorter, a matter of days rather than several months. A few wagon trains still traveled on the trail through the 1880s, and lone wagons rumbled over it into the first decade of the 1900s, but the Oregon Trail has long since has faded away.

Conclusion

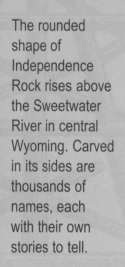

The rounded shape of Independence Rock rises above the Sweetwater River in central Wyoming. Carved in its sides are thousands of names, each with their own stories to tell.

Independence Rock

On July 4, 1824, trappers led by Thomas Fitzpatrick camped by a large granite formation in what is now Wyoming. They named it Independence Rock in honor of the national holiday that day. Clearly visible, the rock was one of the Oregon Trail's most prominent landmarks. Emigrants were always happy to see it because it meant they had survived the first part of their long journey west.

Independence Rock became known as the "Great Register of the Desert" because emigrants etched their names on it. By the time William Kahler arrived July 6, 1852, it was already covered with scrawled signatures and brief messages from those who had passed by. Kahler claimed, "There is at least a million names of emigrants on the rock, some are in small type and some very large."

We Go Westward

"Eastward I go only by force, but westward I go free. This is the prevailing tendency of my countrymen. I must walk toward Oregon. We go westward as into the future, with a spirit of enterprise and adventure."

Henry David Thoreau, "Walking," Atlantic Monthly *magazine, June 1862*

Numbers of Emigrants

Kahler surely exaggerated the number of names he saw. Because no records were kept, however, it is not known exactly how many men, women, and children used the historic trail. Some historians claim that as many as 650,000 headed west between 1843—when the first big wagon train of 1,000 people headed to Oregon Country—and 1869, when the Transcontinental Railroad was completed. Others believe the figure could be as low as 250,000. Most estimates today fall somewhere in the middle, which means about 400,000 emigrants took the Oregon Trail.

These ruts on the Oregon Trail were worn into the rock over the years by the wheels of many heavy, trundling wagons.

The Legacy of the Oregon Trail

Ruts from emigrant wagons can still be seen in spots along the Oregon Trail. They are a visible reminder of the great American migrations of the nineteenth century that helped expand a nation. Some historians believe that, without the Oregon Trail, areas of western North America might never have become part of the United States—that even today, California might be ruled by Mexico, and Oregon and Washington would be part of Canada. Because this historic trail allowed many thousands of U.S. citizens to travel westward, however, new areas were claimed for the United States. The Oregon Trail's true legacy is not the ruts plowed into the earth long ago by passing wagons, but the states and communities that grew up around the emigrants who followed the trail west.

Time Line

1778	March: British Captain James Cook lands on the Oregon coast.
1792	May 11: Robert Gray claims Pacific Northwest for the United States.
	October: Captain George Vancouver claims Pacific Northwest for Britain.
1803	Louisiana Purchase adds large territory to the United States.
1805	November 7: Lewis and Clark expedition reaches Pacific coast.
1811	Pacific Fur Company builds Fort Astoria.
1812	October 22: Robert Stuart travels over and names South Pass.
1818	United States and Britain sign Oregon Joint Occupation Treaty.
1824	Hudson's Bay Company builds Fort Vancouver.
1830	Jedediah Smith leads first wagon train over Rocky Mountains.
1834	Andrew Wyeth builds Fort Hall in Idaho.
	Reverend Jason Lee founds mission in Willamette Valley.
1836	Whitmans and Spaldings travel to Willamette Valley along Oregon Trail.
1839	Alfred Jacob Miller's paintings of the West are shown in New York City.
1841	Jim Bridger builds Fort Bridger.
1841–42	A few hundred emigrants travel west on Oregon Trail.
1843	1,000 emigrants travel west on Oregon Trail.
1844	James Polk is elected U.S. president.
	1,400 emigrants travel west on Oregon Trail.
1845	3,000 emigrants travel west on Oregon Trail.
1846	Mexican War begins.
	June 18: United States and Britain agree U.S.-Canadian border through Oregon Country at 49° north.
	Whitmans are killed by Cayuse Indians, sparking Cayuse War.
	First Mormons travel along Oregon and Mormon Trails to Utah.
	August: Oregon Territory is established.
1848	January: Gold is discovered at Sutter's Mill in California.
	February: Mexico grants large areas of North America to United States under Treaty of Hidalgo.
1850	California becomes a state.
1852–1856	Rogue River Wars.
1854	Sioux clash with U.S. soldiers along Oregon Trail.
1859	Oregon becomes a state.
1869	May 10: Transcontinental railroad is completed.
1877	Nez Percé are defeated by U.S. Army.

Glossary

annex: take over and/or add land to existing territory.

colonize: make a colony, which is a settlement, area, or nation owned or controlled by another nation.

emigrant: person who leaves their country of residence and goes to live somewhere else. The first settlers who came along the Oregon Trail from the United States were called "emigrants" because Oregon Country was not part of their nation until 1846.

epidemic: rapid spread of disease that affects large number of people.

Great Plains: area of North America between the Mississippi River and the Rocky Mountains.

immigrant: person who comes to live in another country.

manifest: obviously true and easily recognizable. When white Americans used the phrase "Manifest Destiny," they meant it was obviously their destiny to take over the American continent.

migrate: move from one place to another in search of food or a new place to live.

mission: center built to establish white settlement and culture and convert Native Americans to Christianity.

missionary: person who believes it is their duty to convert other people to his or her own religion.

Mormon: member of the Church of Jesus Christ of the Latter Day Saints, a Christian sect founded in 1830.

outpost: outlying settlement or military post.

pass: low place in a mountain range; a place where it is possible to pass through a barrier or difficult obstacle.

pioneer: person who does something first, such as settle in new territory or try a new idea.

plains: large areas of flat or rolling land without trees.

reservation: public land set aside for Native American people to live on when they were removed from their homeland.

schooner: type of sailing ship.

Territory: geographical area that belongs to and is governed by the United States but is not included in any of its states.

trapper: hunter who uses traps to kill animals for fur.

treaty: agreement made among two or more people or groups of people after negotiation.

West: term used in the 1800s to describe area west of original United States. Once the "Old West" (east of the Mississippi River) had been settled, whites used the term for the Great Plains and the Rocky Mountains and eventually for the area west of the Rocky Mountains.

westward expansion: the process of growth of the United States that took place over a period of time in the 1800s, when the nation expanded from the east to the middle and then to the west of the North American continent.

Further Information

Books

Blackwood, Gary L. *Life on the Oregon Trail* (The Way People Live). Lucent Books, 2000.

Kimball, Violet T. *Stories of Young Pioneers: In Their Own Words*. Mountain Press Publishing Company, 2001.

Moeller, Bill and Jan Moeller. *The Oregon Trail: A Photographic Journey*. Mountain Press Publishing Company, 2001.

Press, Petra. *Indians of the Northwest: Traditions, History, Legends, and Life* (The Native Americans). Gareth Stevens, 2001.

Web Sites

www.endoftheoregontrail.org The National Oregon Trail Interpretive Center has information and pictures, including an interesting section on African-American settlers in Oregon.

www.nps.gov/fola National Park Service web site for Fort Laramie National Historic Site offers information about Fort Laramie's history and about the site today.

www.nps.gov/oreg National Park Service web site for the Oregon National Historic Trail has good pictures and information about places preserved along the trail in several states.

Useful Addresses

The National Oregon Trail Interpretive Center
P.O. Box 987
Baker City, OR 97814
Telephone: (503) 523-1845

Oregon National Historic Trail
Long Distance Trails Office
National Park Service
324 South State Street, Suite 250
Salt Lake City, UT 84145-0155
Telephone: (801) 539- 4095

Index

Page numbers in *italics* indicate maps and diagrams. Page numbers in **bold** indicate other illustrations.